COUNTRY LIFE
IN AMERICA

It's good to live in the country
Beneath the clear, blue sky,
To feel the wind upon your face
And watch the clouds roll by,
The hush and still of morning
Within a quiet place,
To know the joys of eventide
As sunset lights your face.

It's good to live in the country
So very close to God,
To walk a lovely springtime path
And feel the earth's green sod,
The rain that falls in April,
December's glistening snow,
A summer breeze in August,
October's golden glow.

Garnett Ann Schultz

IDEALS PUBLISHING CORPORATION
NASHVILLE, TENNESSEE

ACKNOWLEDGMENTS

A LIGHT EXISTS IN SPRING by Emily Dickinson, reprinted by permission of the publishers and the Trustees of Amherst College from *THE POEMS OF EMILY DICKINSON*, Thomas H. Johnson, ed., Cambridge, Mass.: The Belknap Press of Harvard University Press, Copyright 1951, © 1955, 1979, 1983 by the President and Fellows of Harvard College. THE GIFT OUTRIGHT and THE PASTURE from *THE POETRY OF ROBERT FROST* edited by Edward Connery Lathem. Copyright 1939, © 1967, 1969 by Holt, Rinehart and Winston. Copyright 1942 by Robert Frost. Copyright © 1970 by Lesley Frost Ballantine. Reprinted by permission of Henry Holt and Company, Inc. Excerpts from *O PIONEERS* by Willa Cather, reprinted by permission of Houghton Mifflin Company. AN ACTUAL NOON DINNER IN THE OZARKS and A BOUQUET OF WILD FLOWERS, reprinted from *A LITTLE HOUSE SAMPLER*, by Laura Ingalls Wilder and Rose Wilder Lane, edited by William T. Anderson, by permission of University of Nebraska Press. Copyright © 1988 by the University of Nebraska Press. THE FIRST SNOWFALL from *STILLMEADOW SEASON* by Gladys Taber. Copyright, 1950 by Gladys Taber. Copyright renewed © 1978 by Gladys Taber. Reprinted by permission of Brandt & Brandt Literary Agents, Inc. COW COUNTRY from *RAWHIDE RHYMES* by S. Omar Barker, copyright © 1954, 1958, 1962, 1968 by S. Omar Barker. Used by permission of author's estate. SUMMER by Hal Borland, reprinted by permission of Frances Collin, Literary Agent. Copyright © 1957 by Hal Borland. Copyright © renewed 1985 by Barbara Dodge Borland. Excerpt from *LITTLE HOUSE ON THE PRAIRIE* by Laura Ingalls Wilder. Text copyright 1935 by Laura Ingalls Wilder; copyright © renewed 1961 by Roger L. MacBride. Reprinted by permission of HarperCollins Publishers. Excerpt from THE NEW WORLD by Edgar Lee Masters. Copyright 1937 by Edgar Lee Masters. Used by permission of the publisher, Dutton, an imprint of New American Library, a division of Penguin Books USA Inc. IN THE SHADE OF THE OLD APPLE TREE © 1905 by Remmick Music Corporation. IN THE GOOD OLD SUMMERTIME © 1902 Horvley, Haviland and Dresser. MY COUNTRY 'TIS OF THEE © 1861 Firth, Pond and Company. SCHOOL DAYS © 1907 Gus. Edwards Music Publishing Company. OUR SINCERE THANKS TO THE FOLLOWING AUTHORS WHOM WE WERE NOT ABLE TO CONTACT: Jo Curtis Dugan for WHO CANNOT LOVE DANDELIONS?; Ruth B. Field for STITCHERY, STAFFORDSHIRE BLUE, and COUNTRY CHURCHES; Mildred Corson Camp for THE CRADLE; Darlene Workman Stull for ANTIQUE BUTTER MOLD; Dorothy Albaugh for AND SONS; Marie Hunter Dawson for CANDLE HOLDER; Rulon Armstrong Jones for COUNTY FAIR TREASURES; Betty Stuart for A CHILD SHOULD DWELL

ISBN 0-8249-4044-x

Contents

Text copy and photo captions set in Melior; Display type set in Benguiat Bold;
Initial Caps in Caslon Italic Bold Condensed

Publisher, Patricia A. Pingry; Editor, Nancy J. Skarmeas; Associate Editor, D. Fran Morley; Book Designer, Patrick McRae
Color Separations by Rayson Films, Waukesha, Wisconsin; Printed and bound by Ringier America, New Berlin, Wisconsin

COUNTRY MAJESTY

There is a dignity and a permanence to the land—from ocean's edge to prairie heartland—that nothing else possesses.

A Light Exists in Spring

Emily Dickinson

A Light exists in Spring
Not present on the Year
At any other period —
When March is scarcely here

A Color stands abroad
On Solitary Fields
That Science cannot overtake
But Human Nature feels.

It waits upon the Lawn;
It shows the furthest Tree
Upon the furthest Slope you know
It almost speaks to me.

Then as Horizons step
Or Noons report away
Without the Formula of sound,
It passes and we stay—

A quality of loss
Affecting our Content
As Trade had suddenly encroached
Upon a Sacrament.

from
THE PRAIRIES

William Cullen Bryant

These are the gardens
 of the Desert,
These the unshorn fields,
 boundless and beautiful,
For which the speech of England
Has no name—
The Prairies.
I behold them for the first,
And my heart swells,
 while the dilated sight
Takes in the encircling vastness.

Lo! They stretch,
 in airy undulations, far away,
As if the ocean,
 in his gentlest swell
Stood still, with all his rounded
 billows fixed,
And motionless forever—
 Motionless? —
No—they are all unchained again.

WHEATFIELD
Colfax, Washington
Dietrich Photography

THE MAJESTY OF TREES

Washington Irving

There is a serene and settled majesty in woodland scenery that enters in to the soul, and delights and elevates it, and fills it with noble inclinations.

As the leaves of trees are said to absorb all noxious qualities of the air and to breathe forth a purer atmosphere, so it seems to me as if they drew from us all sordid and angry passions, and breathed forth peace and philanthropy.

There is something nobly simple and pure in a taste for the cultivation of forest trees. It argues I think, a sweet and generous nature to have this strong relish for the hardy and glorious sons of the forest.

There is a grandeur of thought connected with this part of rural economy. It is, if I may be allowed the figure, the heroic line of husbandry. It is worthy of liberal, and free-born, and aspiring men. He who plants an oak, looks forward to future ages, and plants for posterity. Nothing can be less selfish than this.

SLIDE MOUNTAIN TRAIL
Catskills Mountains, New York
Ed Cooper Photography

A Roaring in the Wind

William Wordsworth

There was a roaring in the wind all night;
The rain came heavily and fell in floods;
But now the sun is rising calm and bright;
The birds are singing in the distant woods;
Over his own sweet voice the
  Stock-dove broods;
The Jay makes answer as the
  Magpie chatters;
And all the air is filled with pleasant
  noise of waters.

All things that love the sun are out of doors;
The sky rejoices in the morning's birth;
The grass is bright with rain-drops;
  —on the moors
The hare is running races in her mirth;
And with her feet she from the plashy earth
Raises a mist, that, glittering in the sun,
Runs with her all the way, wherever
  she doth run.

Cow Country

S. Omar Barker

Here is a country still unplowed,
Where untamed grasses lift
Their heads on mesas rimrock-browed,
In canyons steeply cliffed.

Here is a land that knows the pain
Of drought and drying sod,
Yet grows again each time that rain
Renews its faith in God.

It is a proud and patient land
Possessed and understood
By men as sunburned as its sand,
Who love and find it good.

Photo Opposite
MONUMENT VALLEY, UT.
Adam Jones Photograph

from
THE BROOK

Alfred, Lord Tennyson

I come from haunts of coot and hern,
I make a sudden sally,
And sparkle out among the fern,
To bicker down a valley.

By thirty hills I hurry down,
Or slip between the ridges,
By twenty thorps, a little town,
And half a hundred bridges.

I chatter, chatter, as I flow
To join the brimming river,
For men may come and men may go,
But I go on forever.

I slip, I slide, I gloom, I glance,
Among my skimming swallows;
I make the netted sunbeam dance
Against my sandy shallows.

I murmur under moon and stars
In brambly wildernesses;
I linger by my shingly bars;
I loiter round my cresses;

And out again I curve and flow
To join the brimming river,
For men may come and men may go,
But I go on forever.

THE TIDE RISES, THE TIDE FALLS

Henry Wadsworth Longfellow

The tide rises, the tide falls,
The twilight darkens, the curlew calls;
Along the sea-sands damp and brown
The traveller hastens toward the town,
And the tide rises, the tide falls.

Darkness settles on roofs and walls,
But the sea, the sea in the darkness calls;
The little waves, with their soft, white hands,
Efface the footprints in the sands,
And the tide rises, the tide falls.

The morning breaks, the steeds in the stalls
Stamp and neigh, as the hostler calls;
The day returns, but never more
Returns the traveller to the shore.
And the tide rises, the tide falls.

NAUSET BEACH
Cape Cod, Massachuse
Fred M. Dole Production

WHO HAS SEEN THE WIND?

Christina Rossetti

Who has seen the wind?
Neither I nor you:
But when the leaves hang trembling,
The wind is passing through.

Who has seen the wind?
Neither you nor I:
But when the trees bow down their heads,
The wind is passing by.

NATURE

Henry David Thoreau

O NATURE! I do not aspire
To be the highest in thy choir, —
To be a meteor in thy sky,
Or comet that may range on high;
Only a zephyr that may blow
Among the reeds by the river low;
Give me thy most privy place
Where to run my airy race.

In some withdrawn, unpublic mead
Let me sigh upon a reed,
Or in the woods, with leafy din,
Whisper the still evening in:
Some still work give me to do, —
Only—be it near to you!

For I'd rather be thy child
And pupil, in the forest wild,
Than be the king of men elsewhere,
And most sovereign slave of care;
To have one moment of thy dawn,
Than share the city's year forlorn.

Snowflakes

Henry Wadsworth Longfellow

Out of the bosom of the Air,
  Out of the cloud-folds of her
    garments shaken,
Over the woodlands brown and bare,
  Over the harvest-fields forsaken,
    Silent, and soft, and slow
    Descends the snow.

Even as our cloudy fancies take
  Suddenly shape in some
    divine expression,
Even as the troubled heart doth make
  In the white countenance confession,
    The troubled sky reveals
    The grief it feels.

This is the poem of the air,
  Slowly in silent syllables recorded;
This is the secret of despair,
  Long in its cloudy bosom hoarded,
    Now whispered and revealed
    To wood and field.

COUNTRY BOUNTY

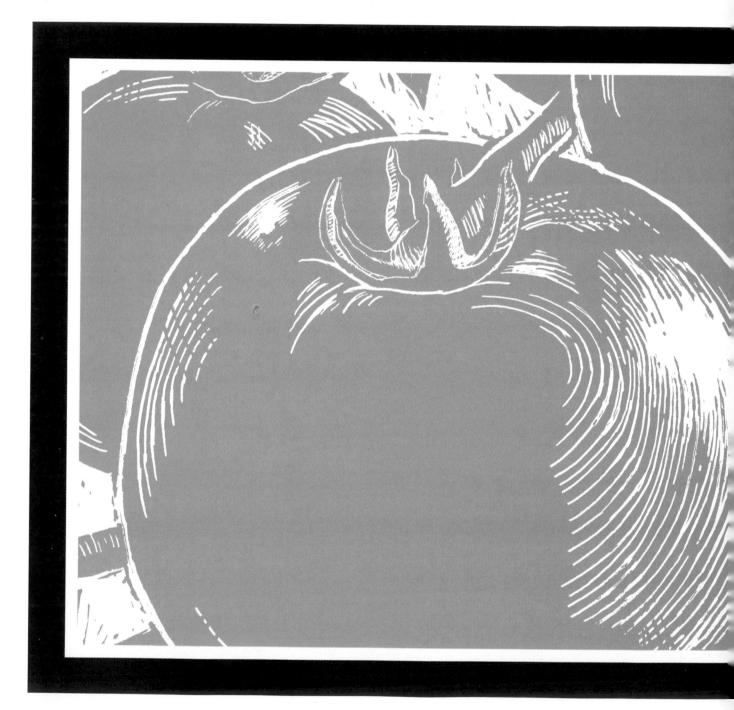

Each year this fertile land—more precious than gold—graciously shares its treasures through bountiful harvests.

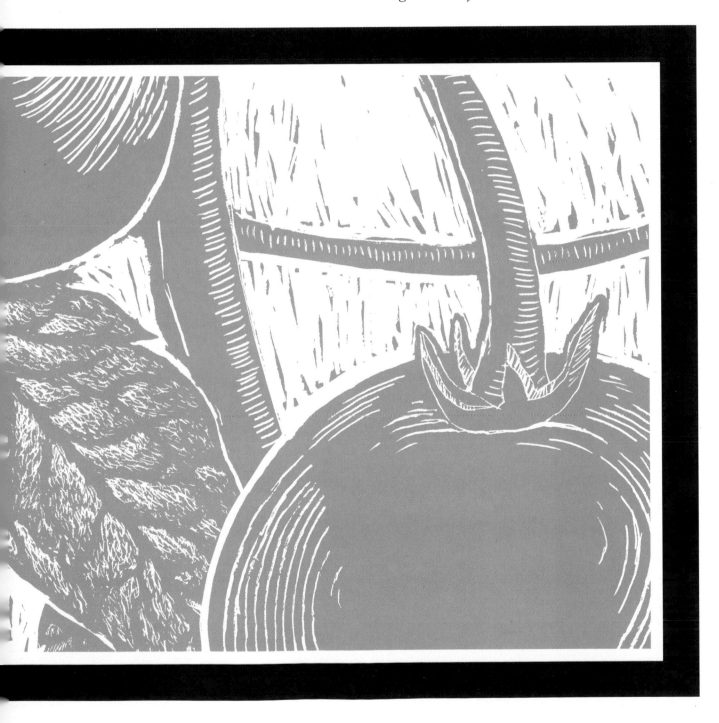

THE PASTURE

Robert Frost

I'm going out to clean the pasture spring;
I'll only stop to rake the leaves away
(And wait to watch the water clear, I may):
I sha'n't be gone long.
You come too.

I'm going out to fetch the little calf
That's standing by the mother. It's so young,
It totters when she licks it with her tongue.
I sha'n't be gone long.
You come too.

GREEN VALLEY
Near Clyde, Wisconsin
Ken Dequaine Photography

If I Were a Farmer

Garnett Ann Schultz

If I were a farmer,
I'd do things worthwhile,
Like plowing and planting
For mile after mile;
I'd tend to the horses,
The chickens I'd feed,
Awaken at dawning
Fulfill every need.

If I were a farmer,
I'd wait for the rain
To give the earth moisture
Again and again;
I'd love all of nature,
A friend I would be
To gardens and flowers,
Each beautiful tree.

I'd plant in the springtime
And harvest in fall;
And all through the summer
My crops would grow tall;
I'd live close to nature
In work as in play,
If I were a farmer
I'd love every day.

WHO CANNOT LOVE DANDELIONS?

Jo Curtis Dugan

There's a lot to know about the dandelion. First mentioned as a medicine in the tenth century, it was being cultivated in Europe and Russia by the seventeenth century for both food and medicine. The early colonists, not knowing what the new land would offer by way of "medicinal comforts"and food, brought packets of dandelion seeds to America. Being adaptable to adverse conditions, the dandelion made itself thoroughly at home in America, literally inheriting the earth. Once here, dandelions went into coffee, tea, wine, and beer and between slices of bread after the young leaves were seasoned with salt, pepper, and lemon juice.

Despite its many plusses, dandelions have been virtually ignored by the arts. Musically, there's an obscure ditty here or there, but none is well known. It seems incredible that Van Gogh types were too busy looking up at sunflowers and August skies to take esthetic note of the gold growing under their easels. Literature contributed little more. Henry Ward Beecher included in his discourse on flowers ". . . you cannot forget if you would these golden kisses all over the cheeks of the meadow, clearly called dandelions." And in Williston Fish's last will, printed in *Harper's Weekly* on September 3, 1898:

> I leave to my children exclusively, but only for the life of their childhood, all and every the dandelions of the fields and the daisies thereof, with the right to play among them freely.

Fish's legacy has endured, though happily his will has been broken by adults, judging from a new understanding of the dandelion that is slowly emerging. Aside from those few who are allergic to dandelions (and that can happen with roses), or the overabundance of dandelions choking essential growth (and that can happen with love), some adults are beginning to view the weed as beautiful. As a grandmother was known to say, "Who cannot love dandelions? They are the first flowers our children bring us."

Though viewed by many as a garden nuisance, dandelions offer a wide variety of taste treats, from batter-fried blossoms to dandelion wine. Many people feel that fresh dandelion greens taste similar to spinach, only stronger, but the earlier the green, the less likely it is to taste bitter. As long as the blossoms have not opened, the green is edible; but if the bitterness is objectionable, reduce its tang by soaking the cleaned greens overnight in cold water with a teaspoon of salt and the juice of half a lemon. Next morning, drain and use in a recipe such as Dandelion and Lettuce Salad. This recipe serves four people. Tear 1 pint of fresh, cleaned dandelion greens and 4 bibb lettuce heads into bite-size pieces. Toss together with 4 chopped scallions, 1/2 chopped green pepper, 1 cup cherry tomato halves; and 1/3 pound shredded Swiss cheese. Add pepper and salt to taste. Top with a dressing of 3 tablespoons salad oil mixed with 4 tablespoons wine or herbal vinegar. Toss well and garnish with sliced, hard-boiled eggs.

Photo Opposite
FIELD OF DANDELIONS
Grand Teton National Park, Wyomir
Jeff Gnass Photography

SUMMER

Hal Borland

A sweet serenity now possesses the land. The struggle is now the measured reach toward growth and maturity. The green world is not fully green. The early rush for a place in the sun is over. Grapes fatten on my vine. Earliest apples show reddening cheeks. The pasture which Albert cut for ensilage is lush and green again. Wild blackberries ripen.

The frantic frog chorus that was so loud a little while ago has relaxed and now only the slow roll of the frog grandfathers echoes drowsily in the night. The brook, so loud in May, now whispers. On ponds and backwaters are large patches of green algae, and cattails lift green bayoneted ranks from the mucky margins.

The heat of midday brings the cicada's shrill drone, one of the drowsiest of all summer sounds. When the cicadas rasp, I know that the insect horde is out of the egg and the pupae and moving toward that stage again. Beetles swarm the grass, ants are on the march, grasshoppers launch from the grass before me as I walk the pasture. Green hornworms gnaw at the tomatoes, strange creatures that in turn become broad-winged sphinx moths and haunt the flower beds at dusk.

The struggle for life goes on, but the great haste of the green world is past. Even in the insect world a balance is struck. It is as though I were being bidden to watch and listen and understand, to relax the little worries and know the big ones for what they are. It is as though I, too, were bidden to strike a balance of serenity.

from
O PIONEERS

Willa Cather

The Divide is now thickly populated. The rich soil yields heavy harvest; the dry, bracing climate and the smoothness of the land make labor easy for men and beasts. There are few scenes more gratifying than a spring plowing in that country, where the furrows of a single field often lie a mile in length, and the brown earth, with such a strong, clean smell, and such a power of growth and fertility in it, yields itself eagerly to the plow; rolls away from the shear, not even dimming the brightness of the metal, with a soft, deep sigh of happiness. The wheat-cutting sometimes goes on all night as well as all day, and in good seasons there are scarcely men and horses enough to do the harvesting. The grain is so heavy that it bends toward the blade and cuts like velvet.

There is something frank and joyous and young in the open face of the country. It gives itself ungrudgingly to the moods of the season, holding nothing back. Like the plains of Lombardy, it seems to rise a little to meet the sun. The air and the earth are curiously mated and intermingled, as if the one were the breath of the other. You feel in the atmosphere the same tonic, puissant quality that is in the tilth, the same strength and resoluteness.

A BOUQUET OF WILD FLOWERS

Laura Ingalls Wilder

The Man of the Place brought me a bouquet of wild flowers this morning. It has been a habit of his for years. He never brings me cultivated flowers but always the wild blossoms of field and woodland and I think them much more beautiful.

In my bouquet this morning was a purple flag. Do you remember gathering them down on the flats and in the creek bottoms when you were a barefoot child? There was one marshy corner of the pasture down by the creek, where the grass grew lush and green; where the cows loved to feed and could always be found when it was time to drive them up at night. All thru the tall grass were scattered purple and white flag blossoms and I have stood in the peaceful grassland corner, with the red cow and the spotted cow and the roan taking their goodnight mouthfuls of the sweet grass, and watched the sun setting behind the hilltop and loved the purple flags and the rippling brook and wondered at the beauty of the world, while I wriggled my bare toes down into the soft grass.

IN SEARCH OF THE WILD GREENS

If you know where and when to look you can almost always find food, free for the picking, growing wild along country roads. Wild asparagus and fiddlehead ferns are two of the more delightful finds. If you are not lucky enough to have access to wild asparagus, garden-grown or even store-bought will work as well with this recipe. And if you can't find fiddlehead ferns hiding under old logs or in swampy bottom lands along streams and rivers, you may find them at your grocery. Just be sure to pick ferns with tightly curled heads, otherwise the taste will be bitter.

WILD ASPARAGUS SOUP
Serves 6 to 8

Pick out about 2¹/₂ pounds of fresh, young asparagus. Carefully wash it and cut off the tips. Drop the tips into boiling water and cook for 3 to 4 minutes or until they are just barely tender. Drain them and set aside. Break off the tough ends of the asparagus and, if necessary, peel the stems. Cut each into 2 or 3 pieces and cook them in boiling water for 5 to 7 minutes. The asparagus should be tender, but still bright green in color. Drain the stalks and purée in a blender with 1 cup of milk.

Melt 6 tablespoons of butter in a large, heavy Dutch oven over low heat. Add ¹/₄ cup flour and stir until smooth. Gradually add 1 cup of milk and allow the mixture to simmer slowly for 5 minutes. Now add the asparagus purée, ¹/₄ cup chopped, fresh tarragon (or 1¹/₂ tablespoons dried), salt, and white pepper to taste to the milk and flour mixture. Mix well and allow to simmer for another 5 minutes. Gradually add 3 to 4 cups of chicken stock until the soup is of desired consistency. Simmer for a few minutes, but do not allow it to boil. Strain the soup to remove the tarragon pieces and return soup to Dutch oven. Add the reserved asparagus tips to soup and allow them to heat through. Garnish with some fresh, chopped tarragon and serve.

STIR-FRIED FIDDLEHEADS
Serves 4

This is a quick and easy recipe that serves four as a vegetable or more if mixed together with rice. Carefully rinse and drain ¹/₂ pound of fresh fiddleheads. In a heavy skillet, heat 3 tablespoons of butter, margarine, or vegetable oil and quickly stir-fry the ferns for 1 to 2 minutes. They should remain bright green and crisp. Season with salt and pepper to taste.

Photo Opposite
FIDDLEHEAD FERNS
Great Swamp, New Jersey
Gene Ahrens Photography

GIVE PRAISE

Beverly J. Anderson

Give praise to God for autumn,
For gold-splashed maple trees,
For gorgeous crimson sunsets,
For woodland tapestries,
For dappled paths a-winding
Around a peaceful hill
Where redbirds in the distance
Glad songs of rapture spill.

Give praise to God for autumn,
For yellow, ripened days,
For bounty of the harvest —
Oh, let us sing God's praise,
For all of autumn's blessings
Are gifts from God above
Who fashioned golden autumn
And blessed it with His love.

WHEATFIELD
Near The Dalles, Oregon
Ray Atkeson Photography

AN AMERICAN FAVORITE

Zana Glass

Everyone knows that as far as sweet corn is concerned, the fresher the better! I know a man who swears that he takes a kettle of boiling water out to the garden, peels back the corn husks, dips the corn into the water and cooks it before he even picks it! That may be the best way to get fresh tasting corn on the cob, but this recipe will deliver that sweet, fresh corn taste without nearly as much bother.

CHEESY CORN CHOWDER
Serves 4 to 6

Carefully cut and scrape the kernels from 6 to 8 ears of fresh corn and set aside. (This should equal about 3 cups.) Sauté 3 slices of bacon over medium heat until done, but not crisp. Remove the bacon and save it to use in another recipe. Add 1 chopped, small onion to the bacon drippings in skillet and sauté until the onion is tender, but not brown (about 6 to 8 minutes). Combine 5 peeled and chopped potatoes with the onion in a saucepan and barely cover with water. Bring to a slow boil and let it cook for 20 to 30 minutes. Add 5 cups of milk, the corn, and 1 tablespoon of butter or margarine. Simmer until the corn is tender (about 10 minutes). Add 1 cup grated Cheddar cheese and stir gently till cheese melts. Add salt and pepper to taste. Garnish with a sprinkling of chopped parsley and serve.

CORNFIELDS

Helen Virden

I like to watch bright plowshares bite the earth
And leave a ribboned row of black sateen,
To plant the seeds and wait for their rebirth
And see the even rows of growing green.

I like to see the fields of corn wave tall,
Then tassel, and turn gold in summertime,
Or see the rows of fodder in the fall—
An Indian village here in pantomime.

Then husking robs the rich, ripe fields of gold
And leaves the broken stalks in lazy rows
Like women, shoulders stooped and growing old
From carrying a heavy, toilsome load.

But as the seasons change, I like the best—
A tired cornfield, white pillowed and at rest.

COUNTRY TRADITIONS

The traditions of country life—passed from generation to generation—grew out of dependence on and love for the land.

THE FAMILY REUNION

Loise Pinkerton Fritz

When winter is past and God ushers in spring,
There's a day set aside for a family gathering.
Grandmas and Grandpas, uncles and aunts,
Nieces and nephews . . . all of the clan
Come if the weather is sunny or wet,
Bringing their families and their family pets.

The chef's at the grill barbecuing the meat,
While the tables are laden with goodies to eat;
The laughter of children is heard everywhere
And newsy discussions resound through the air.
A table with memorabilia is filled,
Including old photos of those we love still.

When winter is gone and God brings back the spring,
The heart longs to go to the family gathering.
A whole year has passed, a new has begun,
And there is a hankering within everyone
To see all the relatives, those new and old
At the family reunion in the cool of the grove.

A Child Should Dwell

Betty Stuart

A child should dwell where there are fields
And farmlands to explore,
Where he can learn the names of trees
And study earth's sweet lore.
Where he can make a friend
Of every barnyard creature
And learn about all growing things
With nature for his teacher.

A place where he can race the wind
And feel the kiss of sun
And walk barefoot in the grass
Or wade in some cool run.

A little one should know a spot
To find the first shy flowers
That blossom in a hidden place
Caressed by April showers.
Oh, if a child can romp and play
In woods, find fields to trod,
He'll learn the secrets of the earth
And catch a glimpse of God.

An Actual Noon Dinner
in the Ozarks

Laura Ingalls Wilder

Laura Wilder was fascinated with Ozark folkways. Even though she and her husband, Almonzo, settled in Missouri in 1894, she never wrote about the Ozarks for her "Little House" readers. She did, however, continually jot down Ozark stories when she heard them and often passed them along to others. This menu comes from notes she made in 1937. She sent them to her daughter Rose some years later.

A Dinner of 93 Different Dishes

Fried ham, boiled ham,
sausage, beef boiled,
beef roasted, chicken, fried,
stewed, and baked with dressing.

Sweet potatoes
baked and fried.

Irish potatoes creamed,
baked, and boiled with beef.

Three different gravies
with meats.

Light bread, biscuit
and cornbread.

Onions, beets, cabbage
boiled, cabbage slaw,
and kraut.

Beet pickles, cucumber pickles,
piccalilli, pickled green tomatoes,
peaches, pears, and onions.

Tomato preserves, crab apple
preserves. Stuffed mangos.
Citron and melon preserves.

Gooseberry, current, blackberry,
plum, grape, peach, and apple,
jellies and marmalades.

Tomato catsup, horseradish
and mustard.

Six kinds of pie.

Six kinds of cake.

"Well set up!" said Uncle Jim. "We haint got much to eat now, but I aim to kill a sheep next week." And the friends he had brought with him from church for Sunday dinner, "set up."

In the Shade of the Old Apple Tree

Words by Harry Williams

Music by Egbert Van Alstyne

In The Shade Of The Old Ap-ple Tree,_____ Where the love in your eyes I could see;_____ When the voice that I heard, Like the song of the bird, Seem'd to whis-per sweet mu-sic to me._____ I could hear the dull buzz of the bee_____ In the blos-soms as you said to me,_____ "With a heart that is true, I'll be wait-ing for you, In The Shade Of The Old Ap-ple Tree."

FISHING

Edgar A. Guest

A day to dream
Along a stream,
The song of birds
Instead of words,
And pictures rare
Flung everywhere.

Instead of smoke
To blind and choke,
An atmosphere
That's sweet and clear,
The trees instead
Of chimneys red.

A patch of sky
To rest the eye;
Instead of noise
A thousand joys;
Instead of greed,
A kindlier creed.

A day to dream
Along the stream
To think and plan,
Restores a man,
And this he knows
Who fishing goes.

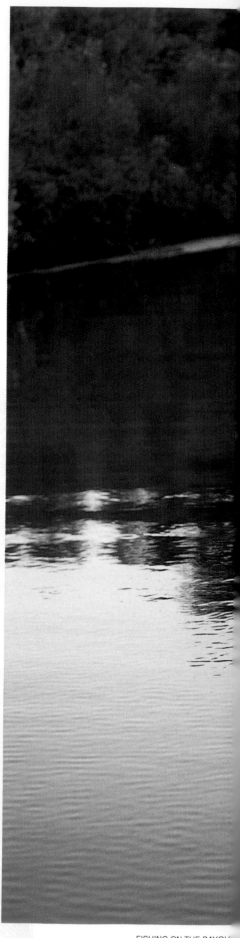

FISHING ON THE BAYOU
Houma, Louisiana
Dietrich Photography

SUMMER EVENINGS

Georgia B. Adams

On a peaceful summer evening,
When the chores of day are done,
We relax on the veranda
Just to watch the setting sun.

All the birdlings are a-twitter
And a soft wind gently blows;
Then it is my tranquil spirit
Such a deep refreshment knows.

God seems nearer in the evening
Ere He puts the day to rest;
He shows tokens of His greatness
And our lives He stoops to bless.

I enjoy these summer evenings;
There can be no better way
When the sun is slowly setting
To relax at close of day!

WHEN MOTHER READ TO ME

Mrs. Paul E. King

At evening when the fires were lit,
When lights were burning bright,
I snuggled up in Mother's lap,
A carefree little sprite.
My head I pillowed on her breast,
From cares my mind was free;
I found the moments too divine
When Mother read to me.

She read me tales of far-off lands,
Of pretty fairies, gay,
And of the goblins that come round
On every Halloween Day.
I was carried on a ship to Spain
Or to a mountain high
Where I could touch the fleecy clouds
That drifted idly by.

I sailed the wild, tempestuous sea,
And scaled Mount Shasta's height;
I even hunted wild elephants
In Africa at night.
Oh! I'd go clear around the world
From Mother's lap . . . you see,
I was a brave adventurer
When Mother read to me.

HARVEST MAGIC

Mamie Ozburn Odum

Harvest days are filled with magic,
All the earth seems ripe and round,
And the yellow rustling fodder
Sighs as cornstalks are cut down.

Every ear of corn is gathered,
Filling cribs to overflow;
Taste the tang of ripened apples
With their red skins all aglow.

Harvest days accompany autumn
With chestnuts falling fat and round,
And yellow pumpkins resting plump
Like golden balls upon the ground.

Oh, the russet and the scarlet
Dress the trees along with gold,
Their gay aprons filled with magic;
Same old story, new yet old.

Harvest days are filled with magic,
The richest gifts come from the sod;
With the harvest comes Thanksgiving
As we kneel in thanks to God.

from
SONG OF MYSELF

Walt Whitman

The big doors of the country barn
  stand open and ready,
The dried grass of the harvest-time
  loads the slow-drawn wagon,
The clear light plays on the brown gray
  and green intertinged,
The armfuls are pack'd to the sagging mow.

I am there, I help, I came
  stretch'd atop of the load,
I felt its soft jolts, one leg reclined on the other,
I jump from the cross-beams
  and seize the clover and timothy,
And roll head over heels
  and tangle my hair full of wisps.

Photo Opposite
HAY WAGON
Near Jackson, Wyoming
Bob Firth/International Stock Ph

THANKSGIVING TRADITIONS

Bessie Replogle

To most people, Thanksgiving dinner calls for a turkey; but my father always said that we should be thankful for what the sea, land, and sky of this great country provided. So our traditional Thanksgiving dinner always included from the sea, oyster stew; from the land, plenty of freshly harvested vegetables; and from the sky, duck! Obviously the turkey is a bird too, but Father said that he never saw a turkey fly, so duck it was for us. Ducks can vary greatly in size, from small teals to the larger mallards, so adjust the amount of seasoning and stuffing in the following recipe to match the size of the duck you have available. Domestic ducks average 3 to 4 pounds.

ROAST DUCK
Serves 4

Preheat the oven to 375°. Rinse two 3-to 4-pound ducks thoroughly and dry well with paper towels. Rub the cavities with half a lemon and stuff loosely with Wild Rice Dressing. Truss the ducks by closing the opening with skewers or sewing with string. Season with salt and pepper. Place the ducks on a rack in a shallow baking pan. Bake for 60 to 90 minutes or until the internal temperature reaches 190° for well-done duck. Reduce the oven temperature to 300°. Remove the ducks to a hot platter, cover loosely with foil, and return to the oven to keep warm.

Add 1½ cups chicken stock and a pinch of dried thyme to the pan and place over medium-high heat. Stir, scraping the brown, crusty bits from the bottom of the pan and cook until the sauce is reduced and well seasoned (about 2 minutes). Strain and serve over slices of the duck with the dressing.

WILD RICE DRESSING
Makes about 5 cups

Rinse 1 cup wild rice thoroughly under running water. Bring a large pot of salted water to boil, add the rice, and boil until tender, about 45 minutes. Drain at once, and keep warm.

In the meantime heat 2 tablespoons water and 2 tablespoons butter or margarine in a skillet; add 3 chopped shallots (or one medium onion, finely chopped) and sauté until softened but not browned. Add 1 pound sliced, fresh mushrooms and 3 tablespoons butter or margarine. Cook for another 2 to 3 minutes. Do not brown mushrooms. Add the mushroom mixture to the wild rice. Season with salt and pepper to taste. Add another tablespoon of butter if desired and mix well.

THE FIRST SNOWFALL

Gladys Taber

No matter in what state our world is, Christmas comes round again to renew our belief in brotherhood and peace and give us hope.

When I was growing up, we used to pack the gifts in baskets and carry them around the little town late Christmas Eve—meaning between five and seven. How I loved those snowy walks with a basket filled with red and gold and green packages. I always think of it now when most presents mean standing in line at the post office. Mama used to tie sprigs of holly in the ribbons.

The snow falls so softly, with such tranquil flakes. It is the quietest thing in all the world, except perhaps the midnight moon on still summer water. Around Thanksgiving we may get snow, usually a scurry of clouds and whirling light frothy snow. But the week before Christmas we begin to see the sky colored like the breast of a sea gull, and the air has an intensity about it as dark falls sudden and soon.

Then one day it comes, first one starry flake, then a few more, and whiteness silently fills the whole air. Now it is really snowing!

I like to get the tree up early, for it is so beautiful and the holidays are so short any way. And if the cut end is placed in water to which half a cupful of blackstrap molasses has been added, the needles keep fresh and stay on the branches a long time.

The tree, too, is a symbol. How good the scent of pine, how bright the fragile gold and blue glass balls, how shining the tinsel and the delicate glass icicles! But this tree, this year, as the tree my mother used to trim on long-ago Christmas Eves, has a meaning beyond any individual tree. It is a symbol of the rich growth which Nature gives us all—out of the dark and frozen earth under the snow came the seed, comes the lifting spire of green. Unless we destroy her, the earth will grow green in spring, bear in summer, glow in autumn, and dream in winter. The seasons with their infinite splendor will roll on; the glory of the sun and moon will be vouchsafed to us. This is the promise of my Christmas tree.

When the moon comes up over the snow on Christmas Eve, I think the world was never so beautiful. The yard is ribboned with long delft-blue shadows and patterned by flying cocker paws. The house has every window lighted extravagantly—for Christmas comes but once a year.

Photo Opposite
WINTER STREAM
Brownsville, Vermont
Gene Ahrens Photography

SLEIGH RIDE

Martha D. Tourison

Beside the hearth the sleigh bells hang
And wait my touch to sound again
That joyous ring that once we heard
As prancing steed tossed high his mane.

Our songs were gay, our laughter rang
Across the fields of glist'ning snow,
For we were young with carefree hearts
Those Christmas eves of long ago.

"We're going home; we're going home,"
Those singing bells would seem to say
As round the bend to lanterned door
Our cutter sparked its icy way.

And now the holly spray I twine
Between each shining silver bell.
I'm glad I lived in sleighing years
That now in only mem'ry dwell.

from
SNOW-BOUND

John Greenleaf Whittier

The sun that brief December day
Rose cheerless over hills of gray,
And, darkly circled, gave at noon
A sadder light than waning moon.

So all night long the storm roared on:
The morning broke without a sun. . . .
Around the glistening wonder bent
The blue walls of the firmament,
No cloud above, no earth below, —
A universe of sky and snow!

Shut in from all the world without,
We sat the clean-winged hearth about,
Content to let the north-wind roar
In baffled rage at pane and door. . . .
We sped the time with stories old,
Wrought puzzles out, and riddles told. . . .

Our uncle, innocent of books,
Was rich in lore of fields and brooks,
The ancient teachers never dumb
Of Nature's unhoused lyceum.

In moons and tides and weather wise,
He read the clouds as prophecies. . . .

Next, the dear aunt, whose smile of chee
And voice in dreams I see and hear, —
Called up her girlhood memories,
The huskings and the apple-bees,
The sleigh-rides and the summer sails.
Weaving through all the poor details
And homespun warp of circumstance
A golden woof-thread of romance.

Next morn we wakened with the shout
Of merry voices high and clear;
And saw the teamsters drawing near
To break the drifted highways out.

We felt the stir of hall and street,
The pulse of life that round us beat;
The chill embargo of the snow
Was melted in the genial glow;
Wide swung again our ice-locked door,
And all the world was ours once more!

Photo Opposite
SNOW STORM ON FIDALGO ISLAND
San Juan Islands, Washington
Ed Cooper Photography

A Country Christmas as it Used to Be

E'lane Carlisle Murray

Across the shadowed room, still bright
Against the dark enclosing night,
Is a merry fire and curling smoke,
Crackling with mesquite and oak.

In a corner, cool and dim,
Its branches bright with tinsel trim,
Standing straight for all to see
Is the fresh-cut cedar Christmas tree.

Above each door, with ribbons red,
Sprigs of mistletoe are spread.
Soft green leaves and berries white
Reflect the candles' golden light.

Long brown stockings in a row,
Dark against the golden glow,
Hang near the soft and gray ash bed
Warmed by embers burning red.

Children dream while in each toe
A golden orange is sure to go!
And crammed with wonders to the top,
Their ribbed expanse will all but pop.

A top that spins and sweetly sings,
A harp to blow, a bell that rings,
A jackknife, or a baby doll,
A red and bouncy rubber ball.

Between these treasures, here and there,
Pecans and walnuts everywhere,
And brightly striped in red and white,
Sweet sticks of peppermint to bite.

The years may pass and yet they'll stay
And never wholly go away.
I can close my eyes and see
Country Christmas as it used to be.

COUNTRY CREATIVITY

The celebration of the self-sufficiency of the country life creates unique ways of enjoying and preserving nature's beauty.

April in My Own Backyard

Edna Jaques

April in my own backyard,
Lettuce, pepper grass, and chard
Sending up small baby leaves,
While a mother robin weaves
Such a wee fantastic bed
In the branches overhead.

There against the crannied wall,
Clothed in lichen like a shawl,
Little niches filled with moss
(An old clothesline strung across),
There a toadstool white and round,
Like a tepee on the ground.

In the shade bright cobwebs cling,
Mystic emblems of the spring,
Hued like opals in the sun,
Gay petunias one by one,
Colorful as patchwork quilts,
Blowing out like Highland kilts.

Ash and thorn and stunted pine,
Peeping o'er the fence of mine,
Little wildlings, yet a part
Of the Spring's great pulsing heart,
Lawns all green and daisy starred,
April in my own backyard.

Photo Opposite
TRADITIONAL COUNTRY GARD
Near Strasburg, Pennsylvania
Lefever/Grushow
Grant Heilman Photography

COUNTRY SAMPLERS

Helen Virden

Bright pictures stitched on bolting cloth
By awkward, childish fingers . . .
An old New England meetinghouse
Near a plain log cabin lingers.

A needled weeping willow mourns
In lines of blue and yellow . . .
Or cross-stitched mottos give advice
In colors years made mellow.

Sometimes a stalwart, straight-limbed oak,
Bright-hued with woven threadings . . .
Or, sewn in faded silk, the dates
Of births and deaths and weddings.

Country samplers from another age
Created with perfection . . .
The work of patient, learning hands,
We treasure with affection.

COUNTRY PICNIC CLOTH

Ann Marie Braaten

2½ yards fusible interfacing
½ yard cream broadcloth
½ yard red broadcloth
2½ yards green broadcloth
⅛ yard black broadcloth
1 yard cream poplin
1¼ yards needle punch
Matching thread

Step One: Cutting Squares and Borders

From the cream poplin cut four squares measuring 17" x 17" each.
From the green broadcloth cut:
   One 43½" square
   Six rectangles measuring 4½" x 17"
   Three rectangles measuring 4½" x 43½"
From the needle punch cut one 43½" square.

Step Two: Preparing Appliqués

Press interfacing to the red, cream, remaining green, and black broadcloth. After drawing watermelon patterns, place each pattern right side down on the interfaced side of the broadcloth. Trace and cut four each of red, cream, and green watermelon sections. Cut 20 black seeds.

Step Three: Appliquéing

Position the green watermelon sections on each of the four 17-inch squares. Pin. Beginning at the flat edge, appliqué the watermelon to the cream square with a wide zigzag stitch having a fine stitch length. Repeat with the cream and red sections. Appliqué seeds with a narrow zigzag stitch.

Step Four: Sewing Borders

Stitch a short green strip to one of the cream squares, leaving a ½-inch seam allowance. Stitch a second short strip to the opposite side of the same square. Attach another cream square to this green strip. Sew an additional short strip to the opposite side of the cream square. Repeat for the remaining cream squares and short green strips. Using a long green strip, connect the two large patchworked sections, leaving a ½-inch seam allowance. Finish outer edges of the patchwork by stitching remaining strips to each edge.

Step Five: Sewing Front to Back

With right side up, place picnic cloth top on the needle punch square. Place the broadcloth square over the picnic cloth. Pin. Leaving a 9-inch opening for turning, stitch around the outside edges, using a ½-inch seam allowance. Trim corners and turn cloth right side out. Press lightly with a warm iron. Hand sew the opening.

Step Six: Quilting

Lay the picnic cloth flat. Pin around the inside edges of each cream square. Using the longest straight stitch, machine quilt along the inside edge of each square. It is best to begin at the center and stitch outward to each corner.

Appliqué pattern
One square equals one inch

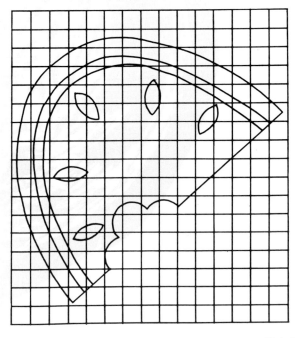

Photo Opposite
COUNTRY PICNIC CLOT
Gerald Koser, Photograph

MAMA'S HERBS

D. Fran Morley

I enjoy growing herbs, just as my Mama did. But Mama had an overflowing herb garden just outside the kitchen door; I have only a row of tiny pots on my kitchen windowsill. Still, when I reach up and crush a bit of fresh mint or sage between my fingers, the scent takes me back home to Mama. Spring, summer, and fall, I could always find Mama working with her herbs and making sweet-smelling creations in her special room.

On the east side of the old stone barn was a small, high-ceilinged room that Mama used for her herbs. Upon opening the door, a wonderful blend of fragrances wafted down from the drying herbs and flowers hanging from the rafters. The early morning sunlight penetrated the room from a small window, giving the carefully stacked old clay pots a warm and rosy glow. Here in early spring, Mama nursed tiny seedlings of curly parsley. During the heat of summer the cool stone room would be a refuge and Mama would be there taking cuttings from her oregano to root for friend's gardens. And in the early autumn, Mama was on the ladder, carefully hanging large bunches of herbs and flowers upside down from the rafters, so that their oils would be evenly distributed throughout the entire plant, thus preserving both the scent and flavor.

Later in the season, when the canning and preserving was all done, Mama would start preparing her special Christmas gifts. For some friends she made elaborate and pungent bay leaf wreaths; others received wonderfully scented potpourri made with lavender and rose buds. To the neighbors and her Sunday school class, she gave deliciously flavored cooking oils or vinegars, spiced with dried tarragon, rosemary, or basil. By the middle of December, the walls and shelves of Mama's herb room would be lined with gifts from her heart. I was always given the honor of tying the brightly colored ribbons on each wreath, sack, or bottle. Then, one by one, the gifts would be sent on their way to brighten someone else's home and heart.

In the cold of winter, Mama rarely visited her herb room. But on the first sunny spring day I knew that I would find her there, working with tiny seedlings and starting the cycle once more. Last fall, even though I had to buy the lavender, I made tiny, sweet sachets for my dresser drawers. Whatever my mood, the scent of herbs takes me back home; and I see Mama again, working in her herb garden and in her special room.

Photo Opposite
DRYING AND POTTING ROOM
AT HERB FARM
Grant Heilman Photography

QUILTING PARTY

Georgia B. Adams

The oldtime quilting party was
A friendly sight to see;
The mothers and the grandmothers
Came from the community.

They spent their time a-quilting,
Oh, how the needles flew!
And oh, what lovely patterns
In yellow and in blue.

They'd talk about their Marthas
And little sister Sues;
(Those were the close-knit families
Who lived by Bible truths).

They'd take time out for tea
And homemade cookies too;
Though I was just a little child,
I joined the grownups too.

I well remember days back when
The quilting class convened,
Mothers and grandmothers met
And made the needles sing!

QUILT AUCTION
TO BENEFIT MENNONITE SCHOOL
Manheim, Pennsylvania
Larry Lefever/Grant Heilman Photography

COUNTRY STITCHERY

Ruth B. Field

Under the silver needle grows
Beauty in color, charming, gay,
The art of country stitchery glows
In flowers and forms in fair array.

Here are the blossoms of the field,
Children and animals captured there . . .
Carefully, then the needle wield
Creating beauty with infinite care.

Rainbow shades and brown and green,
Beast and bud and birds and bloom . . .
All stitched into a charming scene
Lovely as on Mother Nature's loom.

Stitchery picture dreams of the heart,
Lovingly grows each scene benign,
Weaving the new or ancient art
Into a pattern of life's design.

from LITTLE HOUSE ON THE PRAIRIE

Laura Ingalls Wilder

When the Ingalls family was recovering from a serious bout with malaria (what they then called "fever 'n' ague"), Charles Ingalls, unable to work in the fields, took the opportunity to make a rocking chair for his wife Caroline.

He brought some slender willows from the creek bottoms, and he made the chair in the house. He could stop any time to put wood on the fire or lift a kettle for Ma. First he made four stout legs and braced them firmly with cross-pieces. Then he cut thin strips of the tough willow-skin, just under the bark. He wove these strips back and forth, under and over, till they made a seat for the chair.

He split a long, straight sapling down the middle. He pegged one end of half of it to the side of the seat, and curved it up and over and down, and pegged the other end to the other side of the seat. That made a high, curved back to the chair. He braced it firmly, and then he wove the thin willow-strips across and up and down, under and over each other, till they filled in the chair-back.

With the other half of the split sapling Pa made arms for the chair. He curved them from the front of the seat to the chair-back, and he filled them in with woven strips.

Last of all, he split a larger willow which had grown in a curve. He turned the chair upside down, and he pegged the curved pieces to its legs, to make the rockers. And the chair was done.

Then they made a celebration. Ma took off her apron and smoothed her smooth brown hair. She pinned her gold pin in the front of her collar. Mary tied the string of beads around Carrie's neck. Pa and Laura put Mary's pillow on the chair-seat, and set Laura's pillow against its back. Over the pillows Pa spread the quilt from the little bed. Then he took Ma's hand and led her to the chair, and he put Baby Carrie in her arms.

Ma leaned back in the softness. Her thin cheeks flushed and her eyes sparkled with tears, but her smile was beautiful. The chair rocked her gently and she said, "Oh Charles! I haven't been so comfortable since I don't know when."

Then Pa took his fiddle, and he played and sang to Ma in the firelight. Ma rocked and Baby Carrie went to sleep, and Mary and Laura sat on their bench and were happy.

from
O Pioneers

Willa Cather

Alexandra often said that if her mother were cast upon a desert island, she would thank God for her deliverance, make a garden, and find something to preserve. Preserving was almost a mania with Mrs. Bergson. Stout as she was, she roamed the scrubby banks of Norway Creek looking for fox grapes and goose plums, like a wild creature in search of prey. She made a yellow jam of the insipid ground-cherries that grew on the prairie, flavoring it with lemon peel; and she made a sticky dark conserve of garden tomatoes. She had experimented even with the rank buffalo-pea, and she could not see a fine bronze cluster of them without shaking her head and murmuring, "What a pity!" When there was nothing more to preserve, she began to pickle. The amount of sugar she used in these processes was sometimes a serious drain upon the family resources. She was a good mother, but she was glad when her children were old enough not to be in her way in the kitchen. She had never quite forgiven John Bergson for bringing her to the end of the earth; but now that she was there, she wanted to be let alone to reconstruct her old life in so far as that was possible. She could still take some comfort in the world if she had bacon in the cave, glass jars on the shelves, and sheets in the press.

GARDEN BLESSINGS

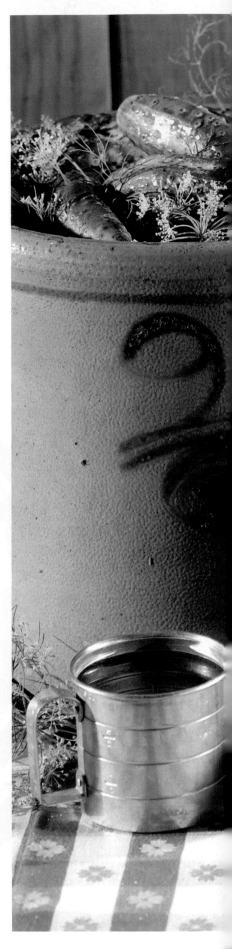

One of the best things about a garden is sharing the Lord's blessings with your family and friends. Here are two recipes sure to be a hit with everyone and there's an extra bonus with the pickles—no salt!

SNAPPY DILLED BEANS
Makes 7 pints

Wash 4 pounds of whole green beans; drain and cut into lengths to fill pint jars. Pack beans into hot, sterilized jars. Into each jar put $1/2$ teaspoon each of mustard seed and dill seed, and $1/8$ teaspoon each of crushed red pepper and minced garlic. In a large saucepan, combine 5 cups of white vinegar, 5 cups of water and $1/2$ cup of pickling salt; heat to boiling. Pour boiling liquid over beans in jars, leaving half-inch headspace. Adjust caps; process 5 minutes in boiling water bath. Start counting processing time when water returns to a boil. Remove jars from water bath; set upright several inches apart to cool.

SALT-FREE DILL PICKLES
Makes 2 quarts

Wash 20 to 24 cucumbers (3 to 5 inches in length) and soak overnight in cold water. In a large kettle, combine $4^{1}/2$ cups water, 3 cups cider vinegar, and 2 tablespoons sugar; bring to a boil. Dry the cucumbers and pack into 2 sterilized quart jars. Into each jar, put 1 tablespoon dill seed, 1 tablespoon pickling spice, $1/4$ teaspoon each of minced garlic and powdered alum, and 4 peppercorns. Cover with the boiling water mixture, leaving half-inch headspace. Adjust caps; process 20 minutes in boiling water bath. Start counting processing time when water returns to a boil. Remove jars from water bath; set upright, several inches apart to cool.

HOMEMADE PICKLES
Gerald Koser, Photograp

COUNTRY EXCELLENCE

The standard by which all of country living is judged has been set by the perfection of nature itself.

I LIKE ANTIQUES

Craig Sathoff

I like antiques—the sturdy kind—
My Bentwood rocking chair
That offers solid comfort
When I am resting there.

I like antiques—the lovely kind—
My grandma's plate collection
Where grand, hand-painted floral plates
Have been her choice selections.

I like antiques—the special kind—
To treasure personally
The shaving mug that Grandpa used
And then passed on to me.

I like antiques—the rustic kind—
The wooden butter molds,
The oaken buckets, iron pots,
And churns from days of old.

I like the charm of bygone years.
I like to hunt and seek.
To put it very simply,
I really like antiques.

FOLK SONGS

Edna Jaques

I love old songs with simple tunes,
And words that common people know,
That have been handed down the years,
And have a rhythm and a flow,
The sound of joyful dancing feet
The rise and fall of a drummer's beat.

Songs of the people gay and strong,
Of lover's meetings, sad farewells,
Feast days and days of special grace,
The sound of holy Christmas bells,
Sounding across the fields of white,
Like angels' voices in the night.
I love the songs of harvest time,
That hold within each glad refrain
The lilt of wind across the hills,
The sound of reapers in the grain,
Stout wagon wheels that lurch along,
The magic of the shepherds' song.

A roundelay, a choir's chant,
Band music floating overhead;
A small girl singing to her doll,
A mother putting a child to bed.
Songs of comfort and of cheer,
That common people love to hear.
Old songs that have a tale to tell,
Of love and joy, peace and farewell.

COUNTRY FAIR TREASURES

Rulon Armstrong Jones

I've been to the fair and what I saw there
Should hold me another short year.
The things on display in such an array
Took tier after tier after tier.

There were fruits and jams and
  pickles and hams
And pastries and candies home-made;
With dresses and dolls
  and quilts on the walls
And satins and linens crocheted.

The fruits of the soil and the farmer's toil
Were the seeds and the grains of gold.
The dairymen, too, had their wares on view,
A varied array to behold.

And out in the pens where the fairground ends
Were horses and cattle and sheep,
And the poultry batch with more eggs to hatch,
And the pigs that were fast asleep.

On the bright midway were places to play
Where the kids were both lost and found.
To make it complete there were places to eat
Where samples were handed around.

CANDLE HOLDER

Marie Hunter Dawson

It may be only a block of wood
With a hole for the candle;

It may be a quaint old brass affair
With a curly handle;

Or silver, embossed, or gold or jade
In design ornate;

Or clearest crystal or china rare
And most delicate.

No matter the holder, the candle it holds
Will melt the gloom.

The same soft light from the taper flows
Till it fills the room.

An Investment in Love

D. Fran Morley

Most people gradually come to love antiques, perhaps inheriting Grandmother's chest-of-drawers, buying a first piece at an estate sale, or strolling into an antique shop and falling in love with an oak table just like the one from great-aunt Sarah's kitchen. However begun, there comes a time when it becomes important to have more than just an appreciation of an antique's beauty. A reputable dealer will most likely not steer you wrong when it comes to making a good investment, but here are a few helpful things to know.

CHAIRS: An old chair will almost always show wear in the obvious places. The legs and the bottom rail should be scuffed and worn from generations of shoes and boots. If the back has fancy, delicate fretwork, expect to see signs of repair or damage.

TABLES: Because the bottom of a table is rarely finished, this is a good place to look for evidence of machine-work (not common until after 1850). A bottom with hand-planing should be slightly irregular. Old table legs should feel somewhat uneven since hand-lathes turned slowly and left spiral grooves that can often be felt or seen with a magnifying glass. Check for darker areas along the edges of a tabletop; generations of hands reaching under to pick up a table results in staining.

CHEST-OF-DRAWERS: One of the best clues for dating a chest-of-drawers is the evidence of use. Check to see if the drawer runners show signs of wear by running your hand across the wood. More decorative pieces show less wear, but there are other signs of age. On a handmade drawer, the dovetail joints will be uneven in shape and spacing. A chest is also a good place to look for evidence of handmade nails and screws. Old nails often had square heads and handmade screws will have unevenly spaced slots. If there are empty nail holes, or if all the nails or screws are not the same size or shape, it is possible that the piece was reworked at some point.

After a few years, a sixth sense often develops for recognizing age, quality, and investment value. Learn the types of wood common to the area, study old pieces at museums and antique shows, and talk with dealers. Check the library for books and magazines about antiques; old catalogs from the early part of this century will have numerous examples of popular furniture styles.

Keep in mind, however, that the word "old" when applied to antiques can mean many different things; and a piece does not have to be 100 years old to have value. A beautiful set of chairs from 1830 might be a good investment, but if an end table from the 1950s has more meaning to you, buy it. An investment based on love is seldom wrong.

Photo Opposite
ANTIQUE WEATHER VANES
Brick Store in Bath, New Hampshire
Henry J. Hupp/Laatsch-Hupp Photography

FAMILY TREASURES

Jane C. Routte

I got the antique linens out
To iron the other day—
And each one told a story,
Had something old to say.
Some are torn, or stained with time,
Some frayed beyond repair,
But each one spoke of dreams fulfilled,
Of loving hands and care.

Some were made for wedding days
And folded in a chest,
And some were made for new-born babes
Held to their mothers' breasts.
Some were made by nursing hands
Working through the night,
And each one tells a story,
Through their stitches small and tight.

I see those women of bygone days
And somehow through the years,
We share a bond of memories,
Of laughter and of tears.
I know they smile approvingly
Because they've come to see
The things they worked so lovingly
Are very dear to me.

THE CRADLE

Mildred Corson Camp

Little cradle, cozy and warm,
Who fashioned you so carefully?

It must have been, that years ago,
A proud, young father-to-be
Walked about his land
In search of the finest tree.

When it was hewn, his task began
With the few crude tools he had
To build this little bed
For the coming lass or lad.

And so for generations,
Babies slept on peacefully
In the little hardwood cradle
Made from the finest tree.

Photo Opposite
SAYNER HISTORICAL MUSEU
Sayner, Wisconsin
Laatsch-Hupp Photography

COUNTRY TREASURES

Agnes Davenport Bond

I have a little table
Of rosewood, I am told,
Presented to my father
When he was three years old.

Its top is highly polished;
Its legs are deftly whorled;
And inlaid work of beauty
Along its side is curled.

I like that little table;
And too I prize it more
Because it came from Boston
And cradles family lore.

I have another treasure
That I like too as well.
It has a task unceasing—
The time of day to tell.

It stands now in a corner,
Erect and prim and high;
And the little Boston table
Is standing just close by.

What tales these two might tell me,
Tales of those olden times—
Perhaps the clock is trying
To tell me with its chimes.

The Antique Shop

Lorice Fiani Mulhern

It was on a narrow country road,
This antique shop . . .
A quaint gray building,
With gables, high windows, and louvered shutters;
And about it an old elm hovered
Like a lacy shawl about its shoulders . . .

I paused, I could not go onward,
For it had a fascination, this antique shop . . .
And a certain warmth
That stirred the imagination and the heart.

Within, it was dimly lit and much cluttered
With *objects d'art* and old relics
That filled tables, shelves and odd corners
And almost obscured its frail proprietor
Nodding over a book and a white Angora.

I found an old oil lamp,
A fine chipped urn,
Mugs, andirons, pewter ware . . .
Parchment maps, a loom, a rocking chair
Among masses of objects wherever I turned . . .
And each in turn my thoughts ensnared.

I mused . . .
Therein the magic of an antique dwelled
To arouse and create a haunting spell;
A bygone world may live again
In rich, yet elusive, fragments.
Each object holds within itself
The charm and mystery of its life.

Photo Opposite
HOWARD'S FLYING DRAGON ANTIQU
Cape Ann, Massachusetts
Dietrich Photography

ANTIQUE BUTTER MOLD

Darlene Workman Stull

I came across a butter mold one day,
Engraved with scalloped edge and sheaf of wheat;
A trademark from the past—the settler's way
Of signing home-churned butter creamy sweet.

I marveled; though the housewife baked the bread
And spun the wool to make her family's clothes,
Created patchwork quilts for every bed
From scraps of bombazines and calicoes,

Although the husband cleared and tilled the land
And worked from dawn to dark to make things go,
Yet someone took the pains to carve by hand
This tool to print a golden cameo,
Upon a pound of butter, worked with care
To grace with beauty ordinary fare.

STAFFORDSHIRE BLUE

Ruth B. Field

Willow-blue Staffordshire, quaint in design
On a lovely old pitcher that catches the eye,
With blue leaves and ferns in artistic fine lines,
Demure little maids play beneath a blue sky.

Linked to this favorite, the cozy room wears
Echoes of blue with touches of gold;
The luster of old wood and blue cushioned chairs,
The present enhanced with the beauty of old.

Copper and brass, a bright braided rug,
Stencils and coin spoons, an old steeple clock;
Geraniums bloom in a blue earthen mug,
A ship's lamp, some trivets, a chair that will rock.

Staffordshire blue has a rare special charm . . .
It brightens the room like a bright blue May sky,
And here in this room that heals like a balm,
I'll sit and I'll dream, then I'll leave by and by.

Photo Opposite
ANTIQUE TABLE AND HUTCH
Gerald Koser, Photographer

COUNTRY COMMUNITY

A special bond connects country families: the common love of the country—of the land itself—and of its way of life.

THE AMISH

When Jacob Amman withdrew from the Mennonite religion in 1693, he and his followers formed a new sect which became known as the Amish. The Amish refer to themselves as "Plain people of God" and lead a simple existence separate from the world. Their way of life is dictated by a strict religious code based upon the Scriptures.

Such modern conveniences as electricity, telephones, radios, and automobiles are forbidden, although the Amish do use natural gas and, thus, have modern gas stoves and refrigerators. For transportation they use the horse-drawn carriage; and horses also pull farm equipment. A horse-drawn combine, however, will often have a gas-powered engine.

The Amish revere the soil; and their creed might best be described by the passage, "The earth is the Lord's and the fullness thereof." Life centers around home, and family members seldom travel far in the course of a lifetime.

Amish use modern medicine and hospitals but first try home remedies. They have their own system of welfare and care for one another with "Amish Aid," each family giving what it can to help a neighbor. At Amish barn raisings, men and women gather for a day of hard work and fellowship, making an economic asset out of brotherly love.

The Amish culture is characteristically one of honest labor, religious dedication, and basic simplicity and their lives are uncomplicated by "the outside world." To outsiders, the Amish way of life appears to be a peaceful, natural, and rewarding experience.

AMISH BARN RAISING
Lancaster County Pennsylvania
Armstrong Roberts Photography

COUNTRY CHURCHES

Ruth B. Field

Little country churches
  so simple in design.
Seem, somehow, to be close to God.
Nestled in a valley,
  steeples pointing high—
A restful place to worship—
This is hallowed sod.

Here old trees sway,
Green meadows stretch,
And distant cowbells ring.
A small brook lends its music,
In tree lofts bird choirs sing.

Within this simple structure,
Built by loving hands,
Narrow pews, a pulpit small
And a small organ stands.
Its mellow strains
  drift through the room,
Quite reverently and slow.
Here country folk sing praise to God,
From whom all blessings flow.

A little country church
Where all seems steeped in peace
Within this sanctuary from all woes
The heart may find release.

DAYS AT THE COUNTY FAIR

Loise Pinkerton Fritz

Time, come take a stroll with me
Back down the lane we came,
Until the "County Fair Days" sign
We come upon again.

Beneath late summer skies of blue
The travelers pitch their tents;
The fair folk are preparing
For a week of merriment.

At dusk the midway sparkles
With lights of every hue,
As refreshment stands and rides observe
The people passing through.

Time, there's so much more to see
But you must go your way;
Because you pass so swiftly,
Sweet moments never stay.

But as the "Fair Days" come and go,
I will remember yet
The memories you have given me,
Too precious to forget.

In the Good Old Summertime

Words by Ren Shields

Music by George Evans

Photo Opposite
FENCE ROW WITH COSMO
Bridgton, Maine
Dietrich Photography

HODGSON'S WATER MILL
Missouri
Dietrich Photography

OLD MILL

Helen Virden

Old rustic mill, moss-covered now,
Dreaming of the past
When large millstones ground the grain,
A trade you thought would last.

A single set of millstones cut
Out of prairie stone,
Rough logs hewn from tall-armed trees
Long centuries had grown.

The whirring mill is silent now
That used to grind the meal;
No rushing water storms the falls
To turn the ancient wheel.

COUNTRY AUCTION

Gertrude Rudberg

Go to a country auction,
And there I'm sure you'll find
All types of people waiting
In one accorded mind.

Both city folk and farmer
Will sit there in the sun,
For hours and hours unended,
To bid and have some fun.

There'll be beds, chairs, and blankets,
Oil lamps and bric-a-brac;
There'll be bureaus, chests, and organs,
And patchwork quilts all tacked.

There'll be pots, pans, and dishes,
Hayrakes, and oxen yoke;
Baskets filled with odds and ends
To make them laugh and joke.

There'll be candlesticks of silver,
Old saws and handmade nails;
Cut-glass vases, braided rugs,
And even milking pails.

Visit a country auction,
And you will get a thrill
If you just sit and watch them
And not your wagon fill!

COUNTRY STORE

Helen Virden

It filled the corner where the crossroads meet;
A hitching rail once stood beside the door,
An old potbellied stove to warm the feet,
A black coal hod to keep trash from the floor.

Here neighbors used to gather every night;
They sat on sturdy chairs with tilted legs.
Here every man could feed his appetite
For news and wait for sorting of his eggs.

This was the meeting place of countrymen;
They waded mud or plowed through winter snow
To purchase from the stock they offered then
Of flour, nails, and bright-sprigged calico.

The store is gone, but I recall the time
When I could buy all heaven for a dime.

THE HUSKING BEE

Ernest Jack Sharpe

A thing once more I'd love to see
Is a good old-fashioned husking bee,
Held in a barn, as in days of yore,
When we all square danced
  on the old barn floor.
When the fiddles squealed out "Lardy Dawe"
"Old Dan Tucker" and "Turkey in the Straw."
Those were the days of good, clean joys
That brought together the girls and boys
And many a romance blossomed there,
As young swains swung their maidens fair.
Old folks sat around side by side
And calmed the babies when they cried.

But all good things must end at last.
The cider flowed and lunch was passed.
Then came good-byes, 'twas time to go.
There were early chores to do, you know.
Oh, how fond memories come to me,
When I think of a good old husking bee.

Photo Opposite
SQUARE DANCERS
Nashville, Tennessee
William Bryan/Freelance Photo Guild

THE APPLE FESTIVAL

Dolly Parker

Every October, folks in our area gather together to celebrate the apple harvest with a festival. To some, there is nothing better than taking a bite out of a juicy apple, freshly picked on a chilly morning, the cold dew still glistening on its shiny, red sides. But at the festival's contest, people all try to outdo one another with delicious apple recipes. There are apple cookies, apple cakes, and all sorts of apple pies, but this recipe has always been a favorite of the judges.

MAMA'S APPLE DUMPLINGS
Makes 4 servings

Lightly grease a 15 x 10 x 1-inch baking pan. Set pan aside. In a small mixing bowl stir together 1/8 cup snipped dates or figs, 2 tablespoons chopped walnuts, 2 tablespoons maple syrup, and 1 tablespoon melted margarine. Set aside.

For pastry, in a medium mixing bowl stir together 2 cups all-purpose flour and 1/2 teaspoon salt. Using a pastry blender, cut in 1/3 cup margarine and 1/3 cup shortening till pieces are the size of small peas. Sprinkle 1 tablespoon of water over part of the flour mixture, then gently toss with a fork. Push moistened dough to the side of the bowl. Repeat till all is moistened. Divide into 4 equal portions. Form each into a ball. Cover; set aside.

Core and peel 4 medium cooking apples. Press one-fourth of the date or fig mixture into the core of each apple. Set aside.

On a lightly floured surface, roll each portion of dough into a circle about 1/8-inch thick. Trim each portion to an 8-inch circle. Place an apple in the center of each circle. Moisten the edge of the pastry with water. Bring dough up around apple, pressing the edges together at the top to seal. Using a knife or small cookie cutter, cut leaf shapes from pastry scraps. Moisten bottom sides of pastry leaves with water and place leaves on top of the wrapped apples, gently pressing to seal.

Place wrapped apples in the prepared baking pan. Bake in a 375° oven for 35 minutes, then brush with the 2 tablespoons maple syrup. Bake for 5 to 10 minutes more or till pastry is golden. Transfer dumplings to desert dishes.

In a small mixing bowl beat 1/2 cup whipping cream and the 3 tablespoons of maple syrup till soft peaks form. Serve dumplings warm with the maple whipped cream.

SCHOOL DAYS

Will Cobb

School days, school days,
Dear old golden rule days.

Readin' and 'ritin' and 'rithmatic
Taught to the rule of a hickory stick.

You were my queen in calico
I was your bashful, barefoot beau,

And you wrote on my slate,
I love you, Joe
When we were a couple of kids.

OLD LOG SCHOOLHOUSE
Strawberry, Arizona
Bob Clemenz Photography

Pot-Luck Dinners

Rose Janczura

At least once a year, usually on one of the first cool fall days, every one in our small community gathers together at the school house for a big pot-luck dinner. Oh, the food there is to eat! I remember so many special dishes, but the one I still prepare today for my family is this one, for old-fashioned chicken and dumplings brought every year by my third grade teacher, Mrs. Prescott. When I married, she sent me the recipe.

Old-Fashioned Chicken and Dumplings
Serves 4 to 6

In a large pot, combine 3 pounds of chicken pieces with enough cold water to cover. Bring to a boil; reduce heat and simmer for about 15 minutes. Skim off foam. Add 1 carrot, cut into chunks, 2 ribs of celery, cut into 1-inch pieces, 2 peppercorns, 1 teaspoon of dried thyme, 2 cloves of garlic, 2 bay leaves, and 1 teaspoon of salt. Cover and simmer for about 2 hours or until chicken falls from bones. Remove the chicken, discarding bones and skin. Cool broth; skim off fat and return to pot.

Meanwhile, to prepare dumplings, sift together 1 cup flour, 2 teaspoons baking powder, and 1/2 teaspoon salt. Break an egg into a measuring cup and beat; add enough milk to make 1/2 cup, beating well. Slowly stir egg and milk into the sifted ingredients. (Batter should be stiff but add more milk if necessary.) Stir in 1/4 cup of finely chopped fresh parsley.

Drop the dumplings by spoonfuls into the simmering soup. Dumplings should just barely touch each other. Cover and simmer for 5 minutes. Turn dumplings and cook 5 minutes longer. Remove dumplings with a slotted spoon and set aside. Dissolve 1/2 cup of flour in 1 cup of water and whisk into broth. Add more water if necessary. Cut up chicken and return to pot and heat. Allow to simmer 1 minute.

Ladle soup into a tureen; arrange the dumplings on top. Sprinkle with paprika and garnish with parsley if desired. Serve at once.

COUNTRY LEGACY

The richness of country life, the fertility of the land, and the generosity of the country people is the heritage of those to come.

And Sons

Dorothy P. Albaugh

It is a proud thing when a man can place
The words "and Sons" above his
    great barn door;
For when his booted tread
    must slacken pace
He comes to set an even greater store
By small bare feet that vainly seek to catch
The rhythm of a stride they cannot match.

And as young minds run swift
    as young colt heels,
He dares to hope his dreams will
    cast a shade
Longer and broader than his height. He feels
A man "and Sons" need never be afraid,
For they and their sons' sons will march,
    heads high,
Across the sweet green earth and never die.

COUNTRY CREED

Lansing Christman

Most of us desire the sanctuary and the peace and solace of the country, the woodlands and open fields. They are such simple things to want, and yet so rich and good.

Open the door to the cathedral of the pines, walk in quietly, with humility and love in your heart. There is no need to seek the remoteness of a wilderness, rather seek a hillside wood, a wild pasture, a meadow or a field, a brook or a stream, a marshland or a ledge on a gentle slope. One does not need a massive cliff of a mountainside. A simple stony ledge will do.

Go by foot, the slow and quiet way, feeling the softness of grass and moss and earth, the fallen needles under pines, the leaf mold under maples and beech and oak.

Walk out into the clearness of the night and look up at the moon and stars. Walk into the light of day. Kneel by a spring and drink of its water without fear. Step out-of-doors to hear again the bluebird in the dooryard apple tree.

These can be yours; but to have them, you must plan with love. You must build with peace; you must harbor with humility; you must walk with respect for your own kind and with nature for now and for generations to come.

PICTURESQUE BRIDGE
Somesville, Maine
Dietrich Photography

THE NEW WORLD

Edgar Lee Masters

This America is an ancient land.
Conquered and re-conquered
  by successive races.
It is the Radiant Land and
  Continent of the Blest
Forever won and forever lost,
And forever seen by that vision which
  thrilled Balboa staring the Pacific;
And forever seen by that revelation
  of the soul which came to John Keats
  through Homer,
For both seas and land,
  and visions of a new day
  may be seen,
And gold may be seen by
  Cortes and Pizarro and their sons,
Who turn all Radiant Lands to gold,
  and starve therefor.
But this New World is forever new
  to hands that keep it new.

FRESH SNOW ON DRY CREEK ROAD
Boynton Canyon
Sedona, Arizona
Bob Clemenz Photography

PROCLAMATION FOR THANKSGIVING

On October 3, 1863, Abraham Lincoln issued this proclamation designating the last Thursday of November—November 26, 1863—as a day of general thanksgiving.

The year that is drawing toward its close has been filled with the blessings of fruitful fields and healthful skies. To these bounties, which are so constantly enjoyed that we are prone to forget the source from which they come, others have been added, which are of so extraordinary a nature that they cannot fail to penetrate and soften the heart which is habitually insensible to the ever-watchful providence of Almighty God. In the midst of a civil war of unequal magnitude and severity, which has sometimes seemed to foreign states to invite and provoke their aggressions, peace has been preserved with all nations, order has been maintained, the laws have been respected and obeyed, and harmony has prevailed. . . .

Needful diversions of wealth and of strength from the fields of peaceful industry to the national defense have not arrested the plow, the shuttle, or the ship; the ax has enlarged the borders of our settlements, and the mines, as well of iron and coal as of the precious metals, have yielded even more abundantly than heretofore. Population has steadily increased . . . and the country, rejoicing in the consciousness of augmented strength and vigor, is permitted to expect continuance of years with large increase of freedom. No human counsel hath devised, nor hath any mortal hand worked out these great things. They are the gracious gifts of the most high God, who, while dealing with us in anger for our sins, hath nevertheless remembered mercy.

It has seemed to me fit and proper that they should be solemnly, reverently, and gratefully acknowledged as with one heart and one voice by the whole American people. I do, therefore, invite my fellow citizens in every part of the United States, and also those who are at sea and those who are sojourning in foreign lands, to set apart and observe the last Thursday of November next as a day of thanksgiving and praise to our beneficent Father who dwelleth in the heavens. And I recommend to them that, while offering up the ascriptions justly due to him for such singular deliverances and blessings, they do also, with humble penitence . . . implore the interposition of the almighty hand to heal the wounds of the nation, and to restore it, as soon as may be consistent with the Divine purposes, to the full enjoyment of peace, harmony, tranquility, and union.

My Country 'Tis of Thee

Words by Samuel Francis Smith

Traditional Melody

THE GIFT OUTRIGHT

Robert Frost

The land was ours before we were the land's.
She was our land more than a hundred years
Before we were her people. She was ours
In Massachusetts, in Virginia;
But we were England's, still colonials,
Possessing what we still were unpossessed by,
Possessed by what we now no more possessed.
Something we were withholding made us weak
Until we found out that it was ourselves
We were withholding from our land of living,
And forthwith found salvation in surrender.
Such as we were we gave ourselves outright
(The deed of gift was many deeds of war)
To the land vaguely realizing westward,
But still unstoried, artless, unenhanced,
Such as she was, such as she would become.

Whⲉn Wⲉ Build

John Ruskin

When we build, let us think that we build
forever. Let it not be for present delight
nor for present use alone. Let it be such work
as our descendants will thank us for,
and let us think, as we lay stone on stone,
that a time is to come when those stones
will be held sacred because our hands
have touched them, and that men will say
as they look upon the labor
and wrought substance of them,
"See! This our Fathers did for us."